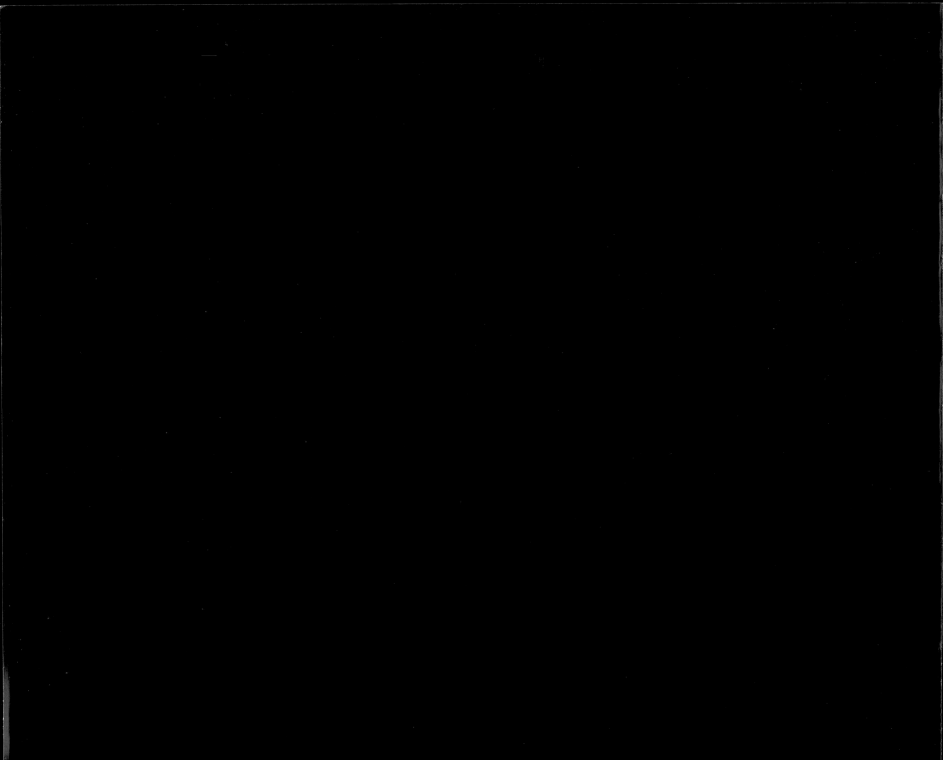

Then & Now

China Photographs

Jan Serr

Edited by Kate Hawley and Jan Serr
Poem by Chang Tsai
Preface by Jan Serr

PLUMB PRESS

ISBN: 978-0-932282-01-9 (hardcover)
        978-0-932282-04-0 (softcover)
Library of Congress Control Number: 2016930336

Editing: Jan Serr and Kate Hawley
Design and Production: Kate Hawley by Design, katehawley.net
Copy Editor: Carolyn Kott Washburne
Proofreading: Paula Haubrich

Manufactured in the United States of America: Burton & Mayer Inc., Menomonee Falls, WI.

PLUMB | PRESS

Milwaukee, Wisconsin
plumbpress.com

For Emily Jonas Hill

Friend,
mentor,
inspiration,
travel-companion

Jan Serr, *Emily—Airport Lounge*, 1996
Ink on Paper, 8 x 4 inches (20 x 10 cm)

The Han Tombs, Chang Tsai, and Arthur Waley:
Translations and *Translations*

In "The Desecration of the Han Tombs," the poet Chang Tsai refers to a legendary conversation between Yün-mēn and Mēng Ch'ang-chün. "Does it not grieve you to think," said Yün-mēn, "that after a hundred years this terrace will be cast down and this pond cleared away." And Mēng Ch'ang-chün wept.

Chang Tsai composed "The Desecration of the Han Tombs" in the third century CE. He is writing about the end of the Han Empire a century earlier. He quotes Yün-mēn and Mēng Ch'an-chün, two legendary figures, who lived four hundred years before that, and who are lamenting the dynastic destruction of *their* time. The poem spans six hundred years and three dynasties, but in the end, the poet says, all is "tumult and disorder," where thieves and robbers roamed like wild beasts, and the walls of civilization are "leveled flat." Of the thousands of possible Chinese poems Arthur Waley could have translated and included in his first book of poetry, he chose this one, about the desecration of a world order. Waley's translations were being made as the First World War was fought, and the book was published in 1918, the year the war ended. Is Waley's "The Desecration" about the decline of the British Empire, and indeed the end of all of the European colonial empires, English, French, Belgian, and so on, and the casting down of that world order? Is it possible that now, "a hundred years" after of publication of Waley's translation, we sitting on the "terrace," possibly at the Kennedy Center, or on the Champ Élysées, or on Potsdamer Platz, watching the current world order being "cast down" and "cleared away"? For us, what is the "then" of the poem, and what is the "now" of this book?

The Desecration of the Han Tombs

At Pei-mang how they rise to Heaven,

Those high mounds, four or five in the fields!

What men lie buried under these tombs?

All of them were Lords of the Han world. . . .

When the dynasty was falling, tumult and disorder arose,

Thieves and robbers roamed like wild beasts. . . .

They have gone into vaults and opened secret doors.

Jewelled scabbards lie twisted and defaced:

The stones that were set in them, thieves have carried away.

The ancestral temples are hummocks in the ground:

The walls that went round them are all levelled flat.

Over everything the tangled thorns are growing:

A herd-boy pushes through them up the path.

Down in the thorns rabbits have made their burrows:

The weeds and thistles will never be cleared away.

Over the tombs the ploughshare will be driven

And peasants will have their fields and orchards there.

They that were once lords of a thousand hosts

Are now become the dust of the hills and ridges.

I think of what Yün-mēn said

And am sorely grieved at the thought of then and now.

Chang Tsai, 3rd Century CE

Translated by Arthur Waley, 1914/18

Of Photography and Viewfinders
Jan Serr

Every medium has its own qualities and characteristics. In music, a piano has a wider range and a percussive quality compared to a French horn or a Baroque lute. In the visual arts, the same is true. A watercolor is different from a woodcut, and both are different from an oil painting. When I make a drypoint, I like to use the characteristics that are unique to the medium, explore those characteristics, learn from them, and develop new ways of working with them—in sum, make the qualities of the medium significant to me and to the work I am making. My arts are tool-based. When I make a woodcut, I have to understand the type of wood I'm working with and the knives that I use to prepare the surface for printing. Then, of course, there is the selection of inks, paper, and printing method—hand-rubbed or a printing press—and so on.

When I'm taking a photograph, I begin by making, consciously or subconsciously, an enormous number of selections and decisions.

For *Then & Now* and *Smoke & Mirrors*, I had to think about where I was going, what I wanted to do, and how I needed to do it.

I had never been to China or India before. I did not know the geography or the language. In China, as in Japan, there are few signs in English, and while many are learning English, especially the young, I could not depend on asking questions or seeking help from just anyone I met. They might have been willing and wanting to help, but the practical reality is that I had to be more independent there than I would in the United States, Canada, or Europe. In India, many speak British English, but there was also the reality of sexual harassment of women, something that I experienced when I was there. I knew that as a woman traveling to these countries, I had to think about my convenience and safety. (I traveled China with my twenty-two-year-old niece, Kate Shannon.)

Early on, I made a decision that I would take photos in public places. That is, I would be a "street photographer." I was not going to be working with a tripod and a hood over my head. I was going to be working in the manner of a group of photographers that I greatly admire: Saul Leiter, Helen Levitt, and Garry Winogrand. I also admire the studio work of Josef Sudek, the posed compositions of Ralph Eugene Meatyard and Nicholas Nixon, and the prepared compositions of David Hockney. For China and India, and for me this time, I would *not* be the studio photographer, but I would be the candid, spontaneous, quick, prolific street photographer.

Consequently, one of my early choices was the camera that I would use. I've worked with many cameras over many years. I've loaded my own 4" x 5" sheet film. I've used an iPhone. And I've used single-lens reflex cameras, shooting black-and-white film, color negatives, or transparencies. These have been variously processed—contact prints, Cibachromes, Kodachromes, and so on. But given the nature of what I wanted to accomplish in China and India, I decided to use a medium-sized digital camera, shooting "raw," that is, unformatted image files with maximal digital information. I used a Canon camera, sized for my hand, where I could effortlessly shoot single-handed. I left my 4" x 5" Toyo and my 400-mm. telephoto Nikon at home.

To me, this is a decision about the appropriate tool for the work I was planning to do. Do I pick up a pencil or a piece of charcoal or a stick of oil pastel? What's the diameter of the pencil, the softness of the lead, what are the options for the paper, what type of lighting do I want, how should the shadows fall, if I want shadows at all, and so on.

In China and India, I worked streets, lanes, alleys, and paths. I stood on balconies, pagodas, and bridges. I worked privately in public places. There are no trophy photographs, the picture that every tourist seeks.

I compose looking through the camera, through the lens. I frame shots. Sometimes I wait a long time for a composition to develop, for traffic to move in a certain way or for someone to turn or for the sun to come out from behind a cloud. I wait, and the composition comes together—or sometimes totally de-composes. Often I take multiple images, so that one of them will be what I want. As Arnold Newman taught, it does not matter how many photos you take of Igor Stravinsky, the important thing is that the "one" is there in the end.

The aspect ratio, the height and width proportions, for both China and India is 2:3. As a painter who stretches canvas or a watercolorist who tapes down d'Arches 14" x 20", I like working with a frame a given size. Using a digital camera, I could have changed the aspect ratio, or, using Photoshop, I could have cropped to any size. But that is *not* what I wanted: it is not how China and India were made. All artists work with a "frame of reference" in one way other another. Marina Abramović sets up a doorway through which people will pass or a square table with two opposing chairs; James Turrell creates an oculus and a timeframe for looking at the sky; Sol LeWitt measures a wall and then describes geometry within it. The rectangular compositions in this book are vertical or horizontal, and of a fixed proportion, my "tuning system" for both books, China and India.

I shot thousands of pictures. This is the kind of shooting that is ideal with digital cameras. I carried three batteries, two chargers (one a backup), and dozens of memory cards. I use memory cards with a relatively small memory, so I'm not putting all of my images on one large card that might be flawed, compromised, or lost. Long term I do not erase my memory cards but keep them as original backup files.

In my studio, I use Lightroom and Photoshop as my "digital darkroom." I do not crop images. Like a "wet" photographer in a traditional darkroom, I may lighten or darken an area or "tilt the paper" to square a line, but basically my work is that of selecting images and adjusting them to reflect what I originally saw.

As I select images for a book, I'm also organizing them in several ways. First, as is apparent when looking at *Then & Now* and *Smoke & Mirrors,* I pair photographs. This is a side-by-side pairing. There may be two vertical images, or two horizontals, or one of each, but I am composing two photographs for a two-page spread, a musical chord. Second, I organize a sequence of photographic pairs. For me, these are visual gestures, akin to a form in t'ai chi, where each section in the book is a complete "movement." One of the most beautiful and instructive books that I have ever seen is *Here Far Away* by the Finnish photographer Pentti Sammallahti. Third, *Then & Now* was composed (selected, edited, and assembled) at the same time as *Smoke & Mirrors*. The two sets of photographs each stand alone, but in another sense, they are a pair of books, Part One and Part Two of a single narrative.

As it relates to the art of the book, it might be good to summarize that again. I begin with a single photograph, which I then pair with another photograph, creating two-page spreads. Then I sequence the pairs into a book. Finally, for this project, I paired two books, China and India. Every step is composition.

I see *Then & Now* and *Smoke & Mirrors* as artist-designed books. Kate Hawley is my collaborator and book designer. We designed the size of the page and the size and placement of the images on the page; we selected the font, the type, the weight of the paper, the endsheets, the headband, the sewn signature binding, and the cloth covers.

When the photographs are exhibited, they will be a different size, and framed. The exhibition curator will select images, all or some, possibly using my pairings, but just as likely mounting an exhibition based on his or her own selection, the size and shape of the exhibition hall, etc. Each installation will be based on the photographs, but each will be different.

One thing, however, will be the same, and that is the concept of "viewer." Let me explain: every camera—optical or digital—has a "viewfinder." The photographer looks through the viewfinder, through the lens, sees an image, and then snaps the picture. With digital cameras, the viewfinder might be a small monitor on the back of the camera that displays the image.

I was the original *viewer* of the image, the photograph. When you look at a photograph, you see what I saw. You are standing with me on the platform of a train station, or the balcony of a pagoda, or the apex of a bridge. You see what I saw, the colors, lines, and composition.

At the beginning of this artist statement, I talked about the tools and materials that an artist has available—brushes, pencils, paper, canvas, and cameras. The lead of a pencil can be hard, making a fine gray line, or soft, making a broad black line. Similarly, cameras have qualities and limitations, for example, in light-gathering capability, the quality of a lens, the grain of a film, or the pixel resolution of a light sensor. In the end, however, when the image has been captured, the film or the digital file does not change.

A photograph is a permanent record of a moment in time. Photography seeks to make time objective, specific, exact, and permanent, which is what unites the early days of Nicéphore Niépce or his assistant and successor Louis Daguerre to Eadweard Muybridge and Harold Edgerton ("Bullet Piercing Playing Card"), or Saul Leiter and Francesca Woodman, or Robert Frank and Stephen Shore.

The permanence of photography is a quality that is very different from the indeterminacy of the drawing or watercolor. A drawing or watercolor involves memory. It is subjective and interpretative. A sketch takes on a character of its own, that is, it changes as it grows; it develops on the paper as the artist works on it. A perfect example of this is Henri-Georges Clouzot's 1956 documentary film *The Mystery of Picasso (Le Mystère Picasso)*. Almost always Picasso begins with one idea, which changes into another idea and then another. He overpaints an area, changing the position of an arm or the color of a shadow. He wipes out an area of a painting and repaints it. There is, in other words, no objective, permanent image, as in photography, but rather an image that evolves out of itself, one mark suggesting another, one color or two forcing the selection of another.

Interestingly, the history of photography, right from the start, was intertwined with drawing. The motivation of Niépce, Daguerre, Talcott, and others to develop a direct, image-capturing technique originated in their desire to improve sketching—to make sketching faster or more accurate. Their journals and letters make this goal clear and certain. Niépce's first successful—but very crude and unstable—photograph is dated 1826 or 1827 Eleven years later, in 1839, the British scientist John Herschel coined the term "photography" to describe the new photochemical process. The word is very telling: photograph, that is, light (photo) + drawing (graphos).

Photographic technique developed very quickly, akin to the development of microprocessors in computers. By the 1870s, there were professional photographers in all of the major cities of the world: London, Berlin, New York, Madrid, Moscow, Tokyo, and Paris.

In April 1874, the French photographer Gaspard-Félix Touenachon, marketing himself under the cognomen Nadar, lent his second-floor photographic studio for the first Impressionist painting show. Among the thirty artists exhibiting in this second-floor loft were Cézanne, Degas, Monet, Morisot, Pissarro, Renoir, and Sisley. Impressionism was a scientific method of painting, photography a scientific way of drawing. They looked out Nadar's window: *it* was their "view finder," their lens, to a new Paris. Degas, always an experimenter, made photographs and, for the first time ever, composed paintings in the manner of a photograph, cropping an image, for example.

Photography started out as a new way to make a drawing, but quickly painting became a new way of making a photo.

Although I am known as a painter and printmaker, photography has been part of my working process right from the start. I make photographs as sketches; I record my paintings as photographs, for my archive and for publication; and I make photographs purely and simply as photographs, such as those in this book.

When I'm photographing, I'm using all of the memories I have to compose, color, and draw out an image.

58

90

100

Photograph Locations

Cover: Beijing (Imperial Garden
       Summer Palace)

  i. Hangzhou (West Lake Park)

 ii. Xian (Great Mosque)

  3. Shanghai

  4. Shanghai

  5. Shanghai

  6. Shanghai

  7. Shanghai

  8. Suzhou (Grand Canal)

  9. Suzhou (Grand Canal)

10. Hangzhou (Six Harmonies Pagoda)

11. Hangzhou (Qiantang River, view from
     Six Harmonies Pagoda)

12. Suzhou (Northern Pagoda)

13. Suzhou (Northern Pagoda/#1 tower in
     South China)

14. Shanghai ("Don't Spit" street signs)

17. Hangzhou (West Lake)

18. Suzhou (Grand Canal)

19. Suzhou (Humble Administrator's
     Garden)

20. Hangzhou (West Lake Park)

21. Suzhou (Humble Administrator's
     Garden)

22. Hangzhou (West Lake Park)

23. Hangzhou (West Lake Park)

24. Beijing (Imperial Garden
     Summer Palace)

25. Beijing (Imperial Garden
     Summer Palace)

26. Suzhou (Humble Administrator's
     Garden)

27. Suzhou (Humble Administrator's
     Garden)

28. Suzhou (Humble Administrator's
     Garden)

29. Suzhou (Humble Administrator's
     Garden)

30. Suzhou (Humble Administrator's Garden)
31. Suzhou (Humble Administrator's Garden)
32. Shanghai
33. Shanghai
34. Suzhou (Humble Administrator's Garden)

37. Beijing (Ming Dynasty Imperial tomb)
38. Beijing
39. Beijing
40. Shanghai
41. Beijing
42. Shanghai (train station)
43. Shanghai (train station)
44. Xian (cloisonné factory)
45. Xian (porcelain factory)
46. Suzhou (silk rug weaver)
47. Suzhou (machine making silk thread)
48. Xian (cloisonné kiln)
49. Beijing
50. Beijing (Great Wall/thumb print ink artist)
51. Beijing (Great Wall)
52. Xian (city view from pagoda)

55. Beijing (Tiananmen Square)
56. Beijing (Forbidden City)
57. Beijing (Forbidden City)

58. Beijing (Forbidden City)
59. Beijing (Forbidden City)
60. Beijing

63. Xian (Great Wild Goose Pagoda)
64. Xian (Great Mosque)
65. Xian (Great Mosque)
66. Xian (Great Wild Goose Pagoda)
67. Xian (Great Mosque)
68. Xian (Great Mosque)
69. Xian (Great Mosque)
70. Xian (Great Mosque)
71. Xian (Great Mosque)
72. Beijing (Beijing Zoo)
73. Beijing (Beijing Zoo)
74. Beijing (entering Forbidden City)

77. Beijing (Hutong)
78. Beijing (Hutong)
79. Beijing (Hutong)
80. Beijing (Hutong)
81. Beijing (Hutong)
82. Beijing (Hutong)
83. Beijing (Hutong)
84. Beijing (Hutong)
85. Beijing (Hutong)
86. Beijing (Hutong)
87. Beijing (Hutong)
88. Beijing (Hutong)
89. Beijing (Hutong)

John Shannon

Jan Serr is a painter, photographer, and printmaker, with work in public and private collections in the United States and Canada. Visit janserr.com or Wikipedia.com.

Arthur Waley (1889–1966), translator, was an Associate Curator of Asian Art at the British Museum, where he studied and wrote about Japanese and Chinese art. In time, he became the single most influential and most widely read English-speaking translator of Japanese and Chinese. Beginning in the early twentieth century, he translated Japanese poetry, Noh plays, and prose narratives such as *The Tale of Genji (six volumes)* and *The Pillow Book of Sei Shonagon*. By the 1930s, he devoted himself almost entirely to Chinese translations, including *Monkey (Journey to the West)*, *The Poetry and Career of Li Po*, and such classics as the *Analects of Confucius* and *The Way and Its Power (Tao Te Ching)*.

The text of this book was set in Optima, the headlines were set in Lucida Grande. Optima was designed by Hermann Zapf for Stempel Linotype in 1955. We see it as a transitional font. While it has the suggestion of serifs—the vestigial brushstrokes of a font such as Times Roman or Goudy—the real character of Optima is its line, thin and thick, which you see clearly in an O or an R or an M, with its planted t'ai chi stance. This is in clear contrast to the line weight, uniform and mechanical, of a true sans-serif font such as Helvetica. The calligraphy of the Chinese ideograph or the dancing glyph of Sanskrit seemed perfect for Optima. Hermann Zapf died June 4, 2015, so this choice of font is thus, in part, a tribute. That said, we used Lucida Grande, a true sans-serif font, for headlines; it's a bit bolder and stands nicely apart from Optima. Lucida Grande was designed by Charles Bigelow and Kris Holmes of the firm Bigelow & Holmes. It was released in 2000, used by Apple for nearly a decade, and is the default body text for Facebook. Charles Bigelow received a MacArthur ("genius") Fellowship in 1982 and has taught at the Rochester Institute of Technology for many years. Kris Holmes studied dance at Reed College, Portland, Oregon, and at the studios of Martha Graham and Alwin Nikolais. In addition to Lucida, Bigelow & Holmes created the munchkin universe of Wingdings.

Special thanks to John Shannon